MEMORIES FROM MY CLASSROOM

MR. REDD

Inquiries and Book Orders should be addressed to:

Great Writers Media
Email: info@greatwritersmedia.com
Phone: 877-600-5469

ISBN: 978-1-960605-47-4 (sc)
ISBN: 978-1-960605-48-1 (ebk)

In the past, the traditional classroom focused on teacher instruction utilizing lecture and paperwork. During class, little interaction occurred between students and teachers. In the 80's, instruction transitioned to encouraging students to talk and interact with their teachers. This new era, stressing interaction and communication, ushered in student and teacher-driven instruction. During this time, instead of simply serving as instructors in the classroom, teachers became facilitators for the children. Initially as a teacher, I perceived children to share strikingly similar characteristics; clearly comparable to one another. Throughout my tenure as an educator, however, each child, despite showing some similarities with others, revealed their real self to be unique and delightfully different. I discovered the truth Antoine de Saint-Exupery shared, "When you give yourself, you receive more than you give." In time, the children in this book, my former students, taught me lessons, gifts that I now treasure. Each became an integral part of me and my wonderful memories. Those remembrances have not only lived in my mind and heart in the past, they remain alive today.

MATURITY

Mariah was a bundle of energy and individualism. With her robust personality, she was like an entire team, just bursting with energy. She was already a young adult way past her years, thanks to her mother treating her as one. I made sure Mariah was given opportunities due to her G/T, top classes, and competitions. Yes, Mariah taught me patience, but sometimes you just know you're dealing with a world changer. I hope Mariah is doing something really important today. She had that much talent.

UNDERSTANDING

Justin was one of those kids you had to connect with for success. He tended to be a little loud and he had his own opinions. I always encouraged kids to grow in their thinking and opinions in a good way, and Justin needed the right kind of teacher. For me, he put it all on the line. He loved science, and was on the best recall team I ever had. He delighted in doing well and I was delighted for him to flourish.

Lesson learned: You must dig deep to understand each child. They are different as snowflakes.

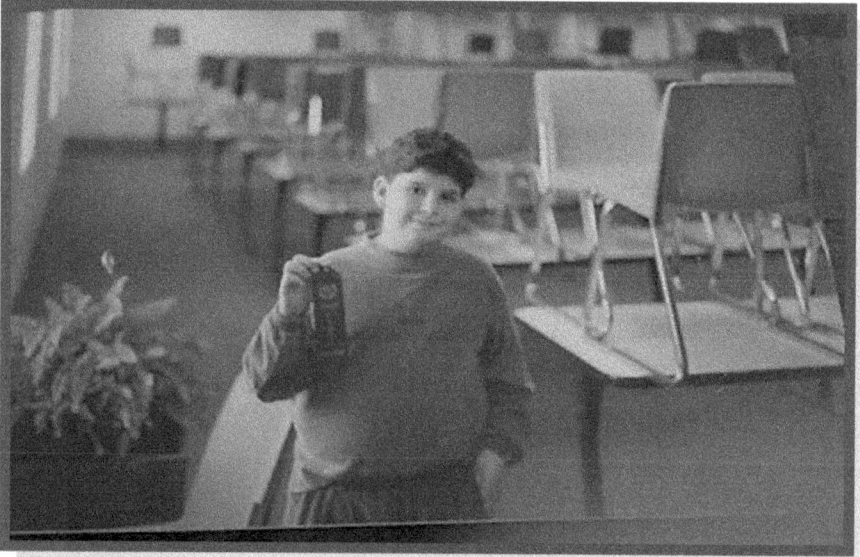

CAPABLE

Aneil was one of the most talented students I ever had. Both right brained and left brained, Aneil could do it all. She could play music and sing as well as anyone. She was creative in all of her projects, and with academics she was the tops. As many teachers know, students that talented are not always admired by the other students. Having that much talent can be a detriment. Students can be very jealous of someone who can do it all. Believe me, Aniel was one of those once in a lifetime students who could do anything. They are one in a million. After a while, nothing Aneil did really amazed me because I knew she had that type of talent.

Lesson learned: Sometimes being gifted can cause another set of problems, especially like fitting in with others.

Aneil could have been a musical star, or anything else she wanted to be. In fact, she still can be someone really special. She had the gift and talent.

AGGRESSIVE

Katie was one of those girls you did not want to mess with, especially if you were a boy. She was naturally very good in sports, and if Katie gave you a certain look, you knew you had better watch out. I placed Katie as captain of our Quick Recall team along with some very well informed boys who knew it all. She ran herd over that bunch of boys, sitting in the middle with her hands out, signaling when to answer a question.

Lesson: Do not underestimate girls. They can do anything boys can.

I hope Katie is doing something to help other people today. She had quite a good personality.

ALL OR NOTHING

Children buy into the mentality that they must be good at everything. If we were all perfect, wouldn't that be something? Katie, with her pig-tailed blonde hair and a smile full of braces, thought she had to be good at everything. Really what's crazy is that Katie had no idea what her real talent was. She was a natural performer, and she had no idea until she started getting up in front of others. I will never forget her taking on the whole gym on a cold winter night.

Needless to say, Katie and I agreed she didn't have to be a great writer. She had other talents.

Lesson learned: Find your special gift and make it your talent. I hope Katie is performing somewhere.

AMAZING

Erin was a member of a special group I had at Collins Lane. Those students all are still etched in my memory and heart. One day, Erin was crying about her performance on the Quick Recall team. I said, "Erin, recall isn't life or death." She laughed and later made the team. But you remember those times when you were truly moved by your kids. I had challenged the kids to do something with shoes. Erin brought in her tap shoes and proceeded to dance along with a song. In later years I saw Erin at KYA, and it made the night special.

Lesson learned: Erin showed me that sometimes students can simply amaze you by something they can do.

I hope Erin is teaching dance to students somewhere.

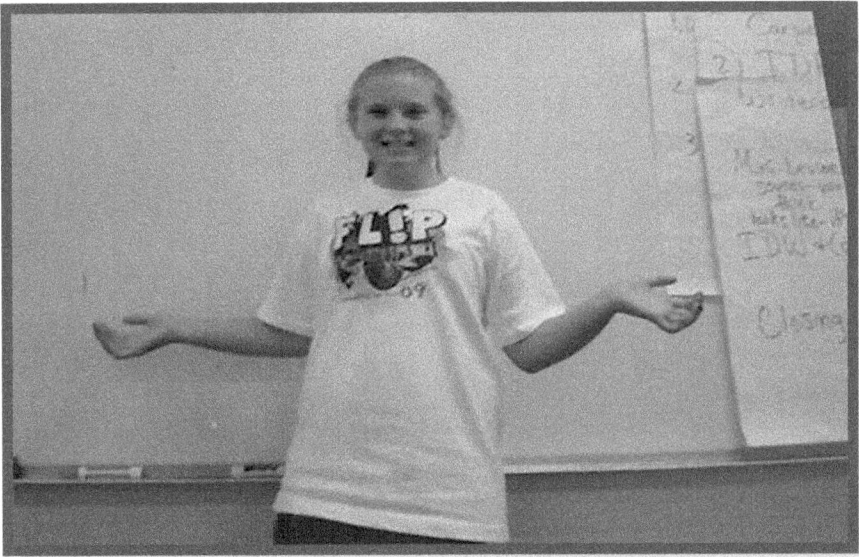

CAROLINE, SWEET CAROLINE

Every now and then you meet someone as sweet as spring.

Caroline was our first granddaughter. She had beauty and a smile that could last forever. Early on with Caroline, things started showing up. She was experiencing trouble with basic skills and walking. She began to have bad episodes, and eventually she had a major seizure. Caroline fought through her illness, and several episodes passed. She now attends school and goes to all school and church events. She never complains. No matter what, I'll never forget her calling to tell me she scored 88 on her spelling test. She was elected Prom Queen for her class. It was a magical moment.

Lesson learned: Caroline taught me you make the best of life, no matter the cards dealt.

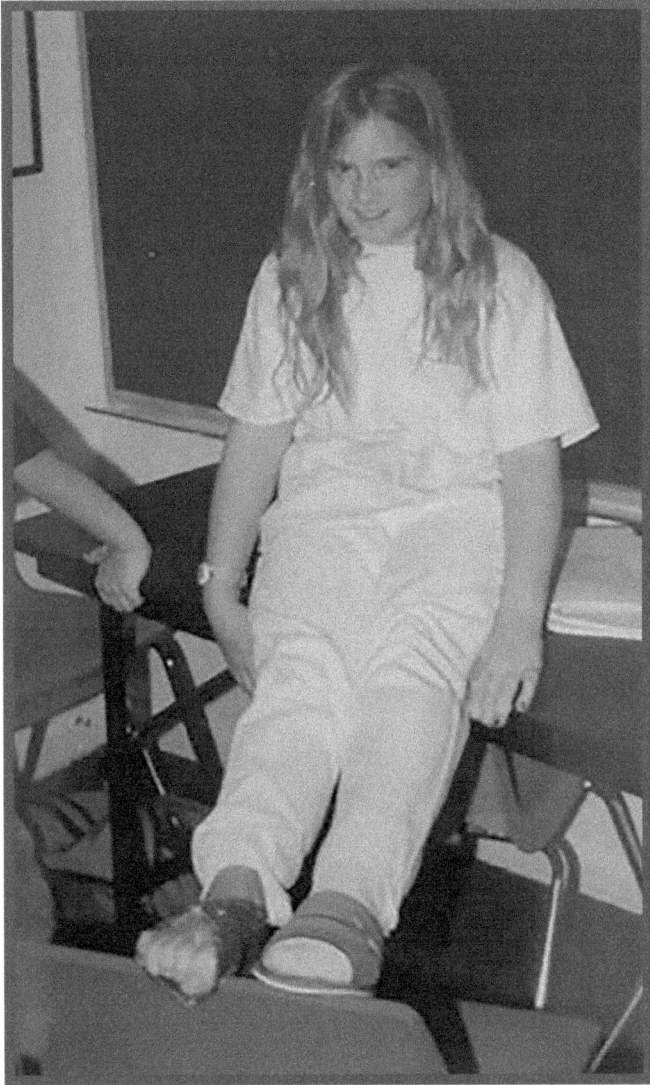

DISCIPLINED

Mary Scott, talk about a child set up for success. Mary Scott knew one direction and it was up. She excelled at everything academic, creative, and musical. She was the type of student you could count on to give 100%. I am constantly amazed what kids can come up with in class. The challenge was always on. Her group performance was a skit behind a sheet with light showing the figures performing a feat. It was amazing. Of course, Mary Scott was my daughter's best friend, so that took some doing.

Lesson learned: With some kids, you do not have to do anything. They are 100% set to go their way alone.

Mary Scott is a doctor now, and I bet a very good one.

DO ANYTHING

Phillip was the type of young man who could do anything, or should I say, *would* do anything. He was confident in who he was and would take on tasks other boys wouldn't. I remember back when I was in college, I was embarrassed by doing a scarf dance. A female teacher told me that day that real men do not care what others think. They have real confidence. Well, Phillip dressed as a girl in a skit as a 5th grader, something few would do.

Lesson learned: Love risk takers that are willing to do something others would not. They are willing to stretch themselves.

DON'T OVERLOOK

Makela was one of those students who demanded your attention. As written in scripture, she constantly tugged at my garments. I finally relented and said, "Okay Makela, I will look at your scores." She had just barely missed the mark. At times, I will fudge things for the greater good. I placed her in our class and she performed wonderfully. She proved herself to me, helping with the stock market game and the Governor's Cup. She was right: She knew that given the opportunity, she could excel.

Lesson learned: Listen to your students. Sometimes you must make adjustments.

I hope Makela is a difference maker somewhere.

EFFORT

Jordan was one of those kids who leaves an impression on you. At first, Jordan really didn't understand the level of effort I wanted from someone. She tried what would have been sufficient under normal circumstances. However, I could see so much more potential in her. She finally rose to the level I had expected, and in fact she was a diehard competitor. My best memory of Jordan was at the 8th grade graduation when she was second. Knowing Jordan, she wanted to be first, but she handled it well.

Lesson learned: You have to communicate that you expect effort beyond the ordinary level.

I hope Jordan is doing something spectacular with all her effort.

ENDURANCE AND CHANCE

Mallory, with her bright smile and brown curly hair, was loaded with endurance. From the moment I met Mallory I knew there was something special about her. She had come so close on all of her testing. I knew I just had to give Mallory an opportunity. She worked harder than most students even think about doing. She excelled in writing something for the Kentucky Derby. She was pivotal on our academic team. Boy did she know her language arts.

Mallory sent me a Christmas card and it meant the world. Retired teachers love past students showing their appreciation.

Lesson learned: Mallory taught me, as they say, to not judge a book by its cover. You need to learn to listen to your gut feeling and go on it for certain kids. I hope Mallory becomes a teacher.

EVERYTHING

Jerome lived with his grandmother and six or seven other children. He was soft-spoken and had a gentleness in his eyes. I took Jerome on as a cause, because I knew I could make my first difference. Along with my daughter, I picked him up for his first Christmas play. Later that year, at a "Just Say No" rally, all the kids bought shirts. I noticed that Jerome did not have one. I took my shirt and gave it to him. On the last day of school, all the kids had a part in our last ceremony. As the kids were boarding the buses and the teachers were waving, Jerome came running off the bus, holding everything up. He said, "You're the best teacher I ever had." My eyes were covered with sunglasses, but beneath them my eyes were filled with tears.

Lesson learned: This was a defining moment in my teaching career, and maybe in my life. It meant everything that I had made a difference in a child's life.

I hope Jerome is doing something that helps others.

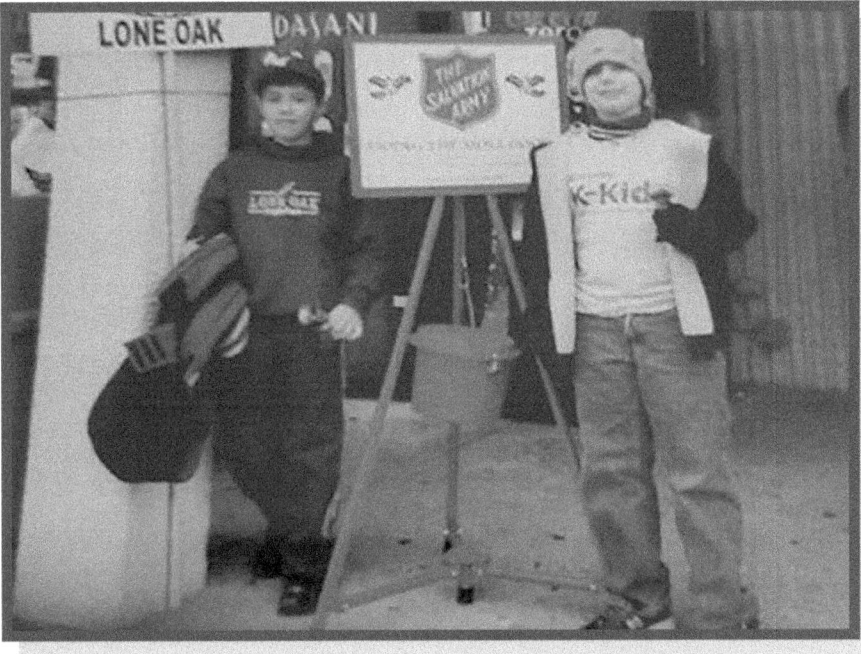

EXCITING

As soon as you walked in the room you noticed Shelby. If you didn't, she would make sure you soon did. Shelby was a beautiful young child with a matching beautiful personality. Shelby could put it up a notch too, once she realized her potential. When it came to acting or drama, she could go all out. Shelby did plays, Odyssey of the Mind, and school functions. She continued to grow with each performance.

Lesson learned: Shelby was one of those just plain fun kids to be around. It makes you so excited to have them in the room.

I know Shelby is performing somewhere in some capacity.

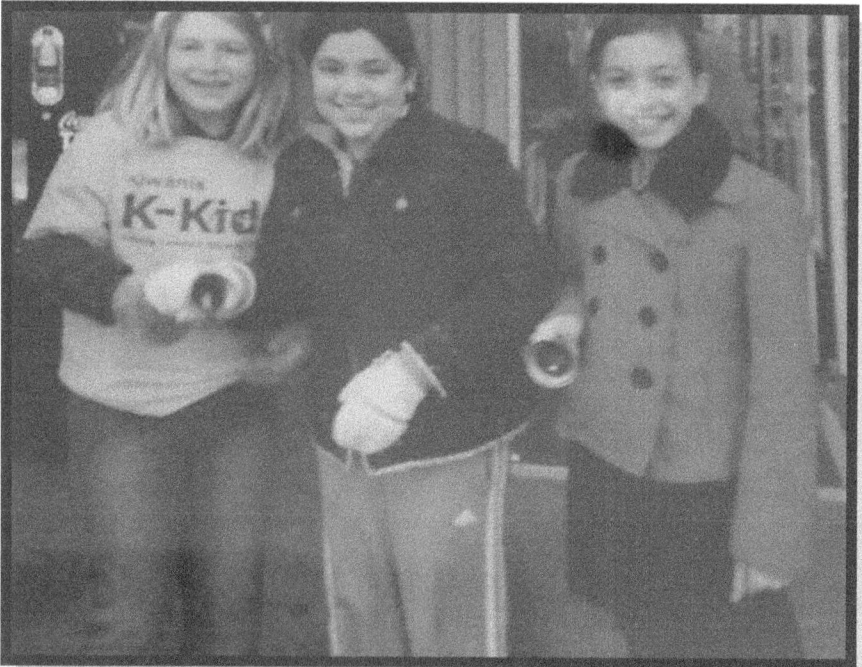

FOR THE TEAM

Warren was a warm-hearted young man who went about his own business. I had to convince Warren to be on our academic team along with someone he did not agree with at all. In fact, they were complete opposites. Warren had to experience many frustrating moments that year, but he was willing to put it all aside for the sake of our school. That year, the school won one of its first academic competitions.

Lesson learned: You must be willing to cooperate with others for success.

I know Warren will do well. He learned a valuable lesson: No matter how talented you are, one must get along with others.

8 .3'95

FUN

Sometimes you remember students for a lifetime. They leave that kind of impression on you. James was that kind of a student. He was Mr. Entertainment daily. James had a manner of making you laugh, even if he was misbehaving. Most teachers could not tolerate the Jameses of this world. Having been a bit of a behavior child myself, I understood. In fact, in moments I had to laugh myself. Who wants a class with no laughter? My wife visited my room once, and James was crawling on the floor with his parka, pretending to be a wolf.

Lesson learned: It's all right to have a little fun at school.

I don't know what dreams I have for James. Well, yes… stay out of trouble.

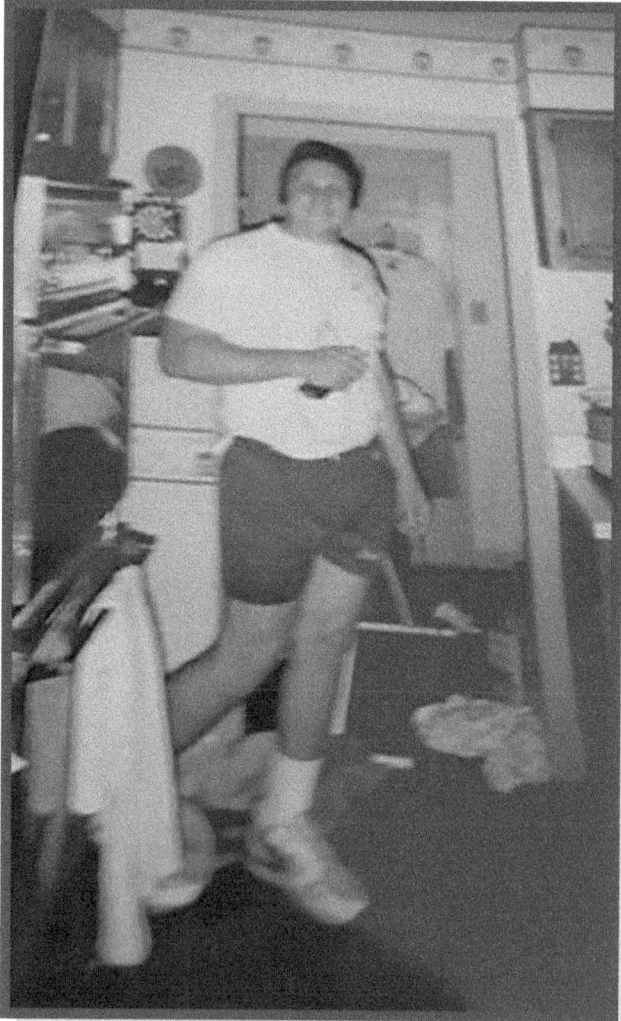

HANDFUL

I met Toby in a different setting and boy he was a handful. Not just day by day, but minute by minute. Toby had a way of getting in trouble without really even trying. For the life of me I do not know why I liked Toby so much. He was all-out boy, and maybe I saw some of myself and my friends in him. We both shared the same birthday. Toby could be a book himself: The real-life Dennis the Menace.

Lesson learned: You can't change everyone, and sometimes you just like them no matter what.

I hope Toby is doing well, and has grown out of his mischievous ways.

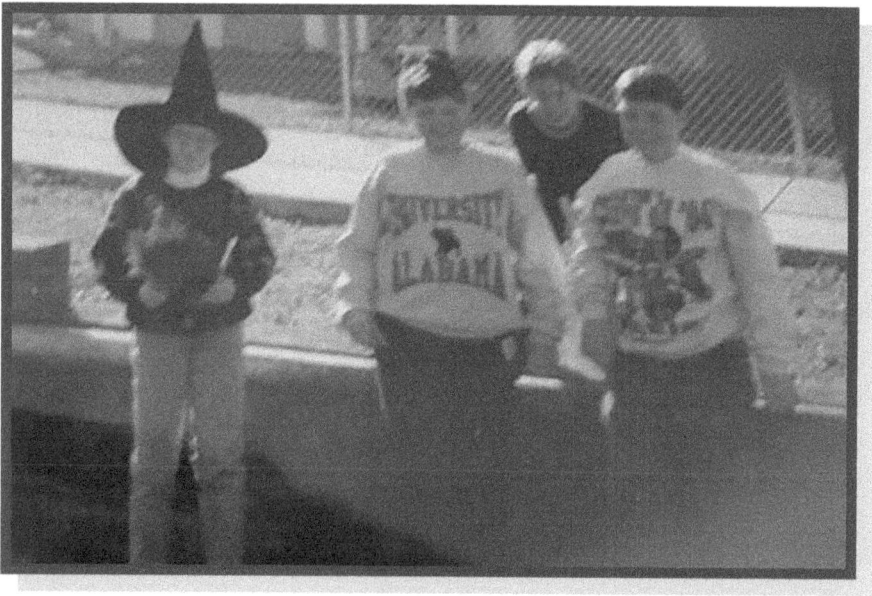

HAND IN HAND

Ben was a red-haired, freckled young man with a smile as big as Texas. And yes, he did enjoy the company of ladies. Ben could have been the next Pat Conroy. He had that natural ability to just flat-out write. However, Ben hated to read, and I never could convince Ben that good writers are usually good readers. I hope Ben still becomes a writer.

Lesson learned: Things do go hand in hand, and a smile goes a long way on a teacher's journey.

HANDLING THINGS

Michael was one of those roughhouse kids you either tame or get tamed by. He could make your class miserable if he had the mind to. I will never forget the first day Michael decided to, shall we say, expel some gas. This really got my goat. I said, "Michael, that was a really nice one, would you stand for a round of applause?" The class just woofed as Michael stood for his accolade. After class, Michael told me, "Mr. Redd, I'll never mess with you again." Michael never gave me another problem after that day.

Lesson: Be different and handle things your way.

I have no idea what Michael is doing now, but I hope he is not in trouble.

INCORPORATE

Rodney was just one of those fun-loving kids, and like a lot of kids, he had a smile as big as a highway. I'll never forget that time during a science class late one afternoon when Rodney decided to add his voice to the lesson. The lesson involved primates, and Rodney cut loose with a chimpanzee noise. Naturally, most teachers would have been annoyed, but I found it just the opposite. So whenever we would discuss our chapter review, I invited Rodney to make his voice connections. The kids loved it and it probably reinforced their learning.

Lesson learned: Involve your kids with the lessons whenever possible. Rodney was the beginning of learning that lesson.

I hope Rodney never loses his humor.

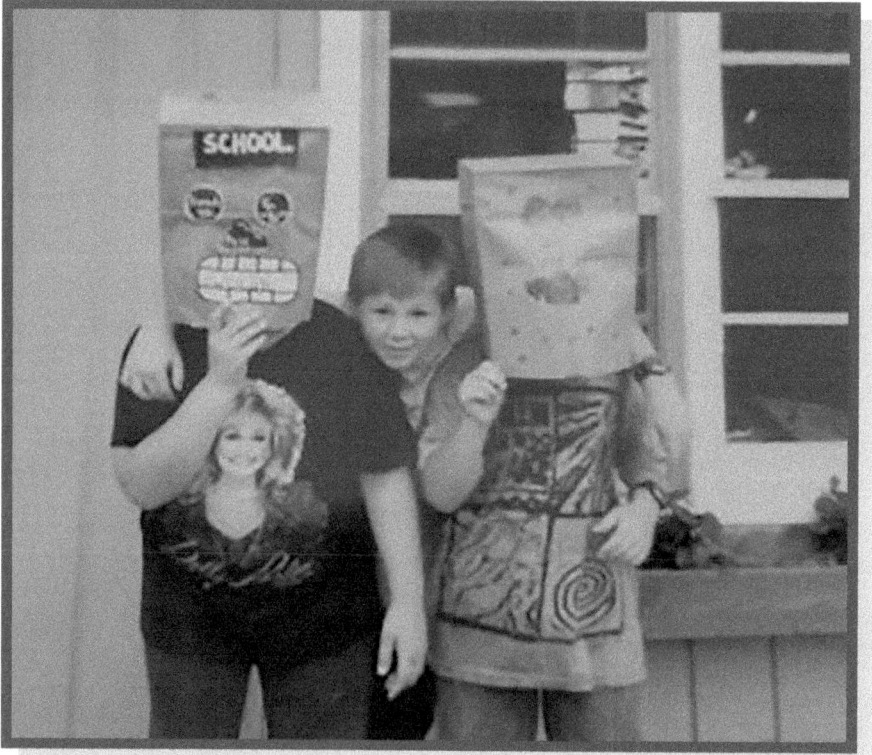

LAUGHTER

Talk about Miss Laughter! Lauren could laugh about anything. I took Lauren to be a speech person, especially with her storytelling. But I wasn't dead on, so I took her to a speech tournament. The telling story about Lauren happened one day while I had the instructor showing children how to do sit-up exercises. Lauren stressed herself a little bit too much and, shall we say, pooted, or more polite, expelled a little gas. Now, most kids would have been embarrassed about this. Not Lauren. She laughed in spite of herself. In fact, the whole class did. That was just the kind of person Lauren was to become.

Later, Lauren became an excellent speaker in college and won many trophies. She married a nice young man who is a teacher. Makes sense.

Lesson learned: You just have to laugh at your mistakes. Lauren, who I am really proud of, is a Christian speaker right now.

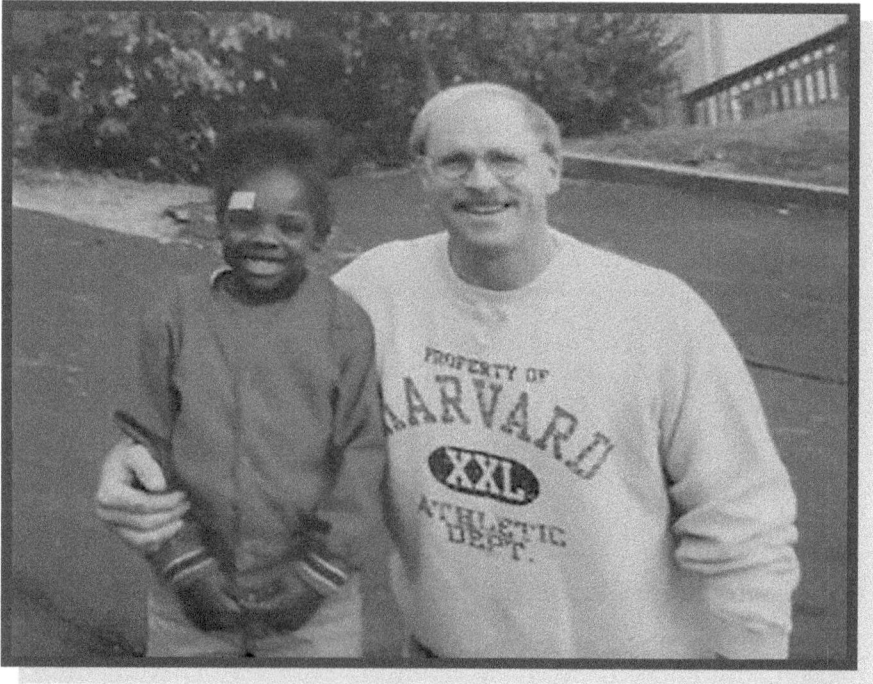

LEFT ON RIGHT

Laney had a strong left brain and right brain: Both hemispheres. You have heard me speak of such children. I had three during my career. They could do academics, creative projects, acting, speech, math… anything. She and Shelly were two peas in a pod. Now if they fought, you knew it was going to be a dandy. But most times they ran in rhythm. They both could act, do drama, and participate in Odyssey of the Mind. Laney could do academics as well as anyone, and her scores were off the charts.

Lesson: Every now and then you get a Laney, Aneil, or Leigh, and you just enjoy the experience. Laney is going to be acting and doing business somewhere.

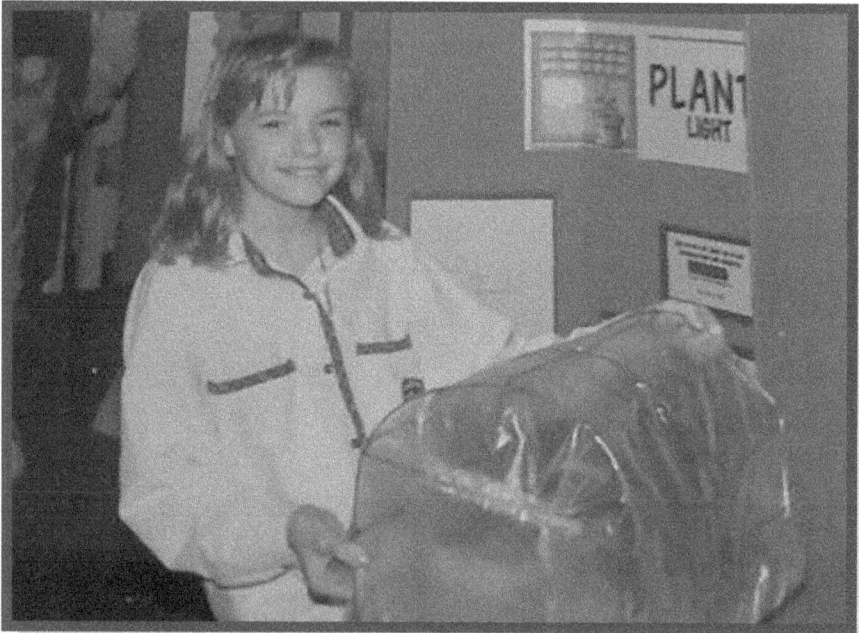

LISTENING

Sheldon was a beautiful blonde-haired child with blue eyes and a voice to match. She came from the most wonderful set of parents. Now I admit I know little about musical talent, but I do know talent when I see it. Sheldon sang at school one evening and I was amazed. I asked our gifted KAGE person if she could sing at the Capitol. This was a very big deal! She sang in the annex, in the Senate, and in the House of Representatives. It was a Red Letter day. Her parents were so proud. I was a nervous wreck.

Lesson learned: You learn never to put your students to a challenge that may be too much for them. You never know, but it's your call.

I hope Sheldon goes to Nashville.

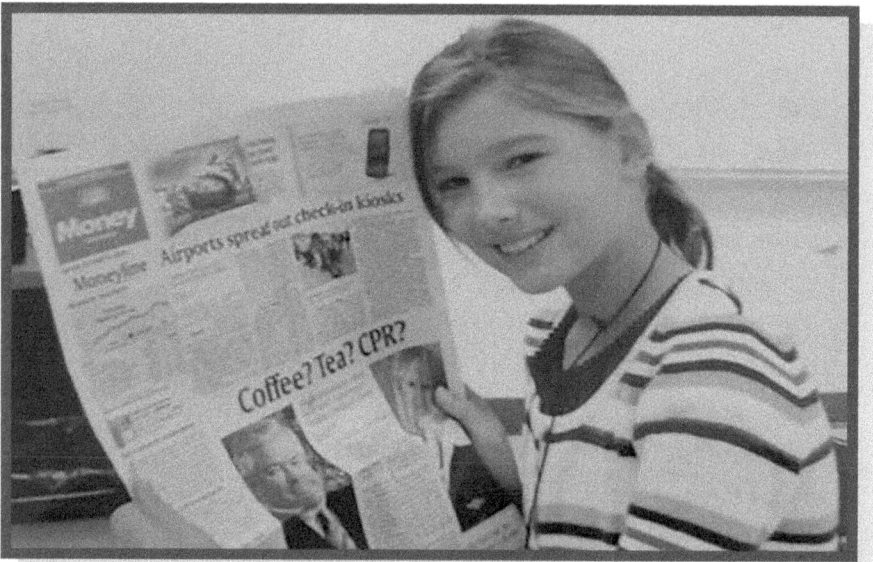

LOSING

G reg was one of my first tastes of reality. I could not for the life of me win him over. Greg was a huge fifth grader who had a bit of anger from somewhere. Greg was tough on the other kids and I had to eyeball him all the time, but I always felt I could reach Greg somehow. However, I found that sometimes you are not able to work your magic, and you have to take defeat. Greg was removed from school for disciplinary reasons.

Lesson learned: Sometimes you lose, and you cannot change all children. Sometimes life experiences have taken their toll, and you must accept you're not Mr. Magic.

I hope Greg is having a good life, wherever he is.

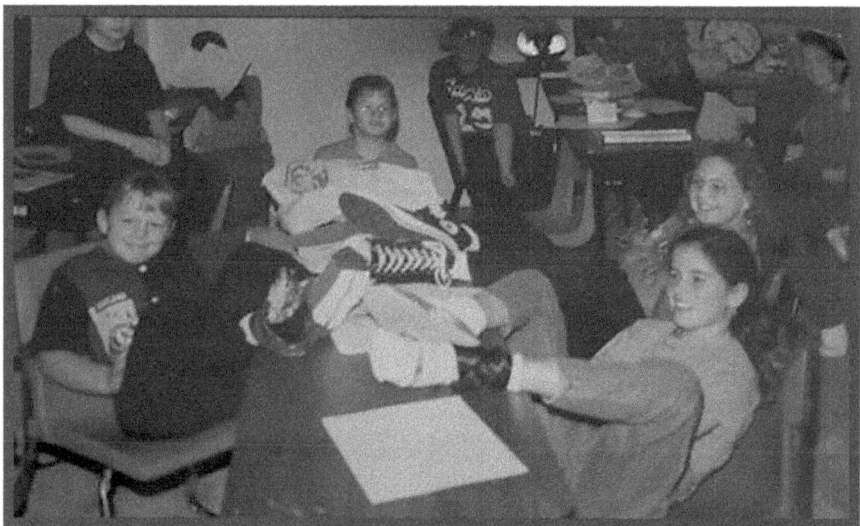

QUESTIONABLE

Mariam was a delightful young lady in my first year of teaching. She was the type of person who could talk all day long. However, she never wanted to be called on in class. She would not make eye contact and she put her head down. Eventually, I knew she knew the answers but was afraid of being wrong. One day in class during my observations, I said, "Well class, I am going for broke. I am going to call on Mariam." The class let out an 'oh no!' but Mariam raised her head up and answered the question. Needless to say, it made my day.

Lesson learned: Don't be afraid to call on someone, even if they have the wrong answer. Do not be afraid to ask the question.

I hope Mariam has her head up and is doing well in life.

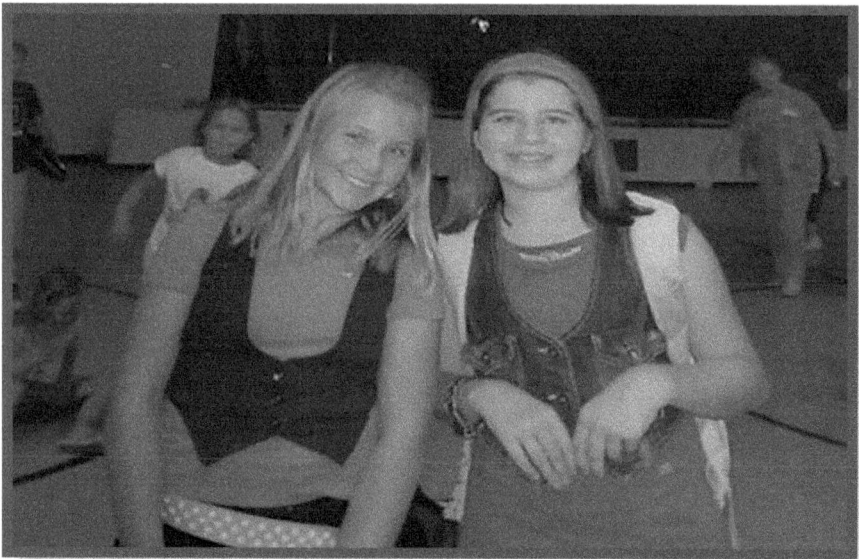

NICE

Allison was one of those kids you would adopt if you could. She had a sweetness and a laugh that filled the room. Allison had a just plain special personality, maybe from the passion she had for life. She excelled in all classes, acting, and academics, but she basically excelled in living life. Her laugh took every bite of oxygen out of the room.

Lesson learned: Teachers, enjoy those plain days because you will not get them back with Allisons in the room.

I have the feeling Allison will be in the ministry one day. She has a special gift, and is a difference maker.

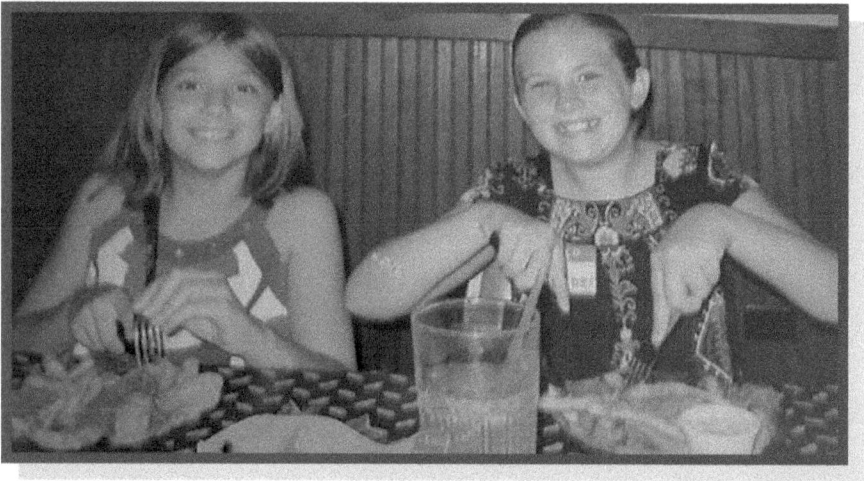

NO

Leigh was gifted right and left, and wanted to perform on all levels. Leigh had the qualities of two other students mentioned: Aneil and Laney. They could do it all. Academics, acting, creativity. Truly gifted and talented. You can have a gift, but it is up to you to make it a talent. She could push herself to the limit. That is, until one day when she nearly passed out in the lab from exhaustion and had to be taken to the hospital. Leigh learned from that experience and placed priorities on her activities. She became much more balanced as an individual and she became an excellent lawyer. She again found her limits and gave up the dollars to have a family and be a professor.

Lesson learned: You must learn to say 'no,' even if everyone wants a part of you.

NON-STOP

Shawn was one of the most active kids I ever met in my life. Shawn had more energy than any mode of transportation. He was a young boy in his zenith. Shawn would do any activity for a few minutes. Basketball, ping pong, games… this was a constant with Shawn. He literally wore you out, and why he and I became buddies I will never know. I guess I always gravitate to kids who are different. In my dreams I can still hear Shawn say, "Hey James."

Lesson learned: With kids like Shawn who have a lot of energy, you must go with the flow.

I hope Shawn has settled down.

QUESTIONS?

Clint was an excellent student in a class of very smart kids. He was one of those good kids who never gave you a bit of trouble. In fact, just the opposite: He always was positive and friendly to all.

Teachers should encourage their students to ask good questions. This is the whole essence of learning. So Clint asked me one day during science class, "Where do clouds come from?" Now, I know some subjects better than others, and science was not my favorite. I gave the stock answer: "Let's research it."

Lesson learned: Encourage your students to ask hard questions, admit when you do not know the answers, and everyone learns.

I hope Clint does well. He was sharp, nice, and dedicated. Again, I would not be surprised if he is teaching. His dad was a great principal and I bet he would want to follow.

REVERSIBLE

Ivy. Never have I met a child that could be perfect at school, and the minute they touch the car, turn from Dr. Jekyll into Mr. Hyde. It always amazed me to hear the teachers brag about what a good student Ivy was, our Ivy. Ivy is one passionate man who wants to do well, and of course he needs some fine- tuning to get to the top. I'll never forget the talk we had during one baseball game when the coaches were really doubting his ability. We had one of those talks about knowing your capabilities. It was the biggest moment in my life, watching Ivy knock a homer in an All Star game.

Lesson learned: Spend time with your kids and grandkids. You do not get those moments back.

One day Ivy will be very successful in a lot of aspects of life.

SO CLOSE

Wes left a definite impression on me. He left an impression on most people. Wes was Mr. Happy-Go-Lucky, Mr. Let's Just Do It. He pictured himself as a professional ball player. Now, Wes was a challenge in many ways. But I remember after one science test, once he had finished the test, he turned the paper over and drew and labeled everything in the chapter. I was astounded at what he could do if he wanted to. He placed second in the regional math competition, and I'll never forget seeing him throw the ribbon into the trashcan. He stated, "We are going to be ball players."

Lesson learned: Wes taught me that sometimes you can want something for the student more than they do, especially when you know they have endless ability.

I wish Wes had pushed himself to his full potential, but sometimes they just want what they want.

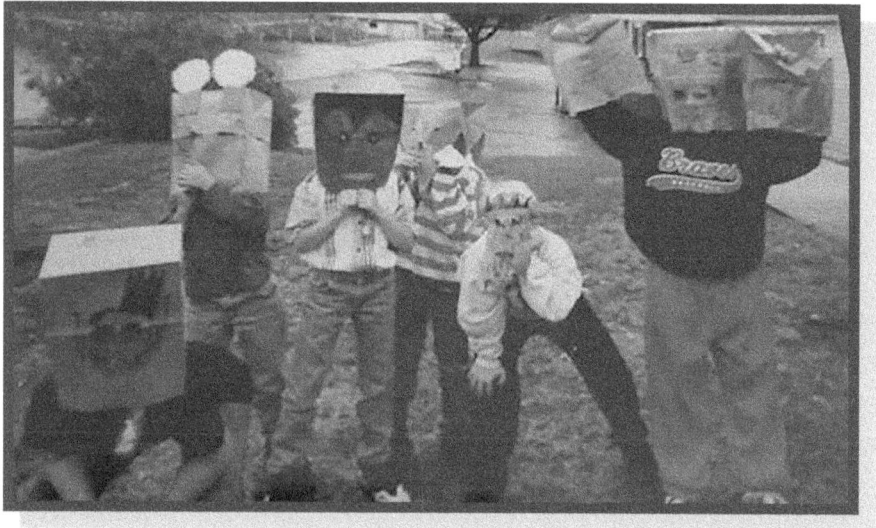

STEPPIN' UP

Caleb was a blonde-haired, blue-eyed boy with a heck of a grin. He had that flash that people can put on when needed. Of course, I saw huge potential in Caleb because he did well academically. He also was one of those kids who believed you when you said something. Caleb was in a state-winning stock market contest that year, and at the banquet I encouraged him to speak. At first he appeared nervous, then he flashed that grin and went into his talk. He owned that room of CEOs. It was a lifetime moment.

Lesson: If you truly believe in a person, they can come back in a big way. I hope Caleb is in business, maybe as a broker.

SWEETNESS

Sonya was one of the sweetest children I ever taught. She had a special gentleness about her that transcended her circumstances. She lived above and beyond her situation. She was well read, laughed a lot, and was a total pleasure to be around. She was like a lot of my kids, with that 'diamond in the rough' ability, that ability to perform at levels beyond others. Not many children can win three events in an academic competition. However, Sonya was one of those rare people who could perform such feats. Sonya taught me you do not have to be above the crowd, that you can be sweet and compassionate and still be successful.

Sonya is currently working at a pizza restaurant. I know great things are ahead.

TOUGH

Aiden was a very challenging student to get where you wanted him to be. Aiden could out-perform anyone in a given subject. His academic knowledge was off the charts. He, like many of those gifted children, had a discouraging or challenging time with others. Yes, you see a pattern here of students having difficulties when they are so gifted. Aiden could be a wrecking crew on academic competition. He helped take the school to first place in the Governor's Cup.

Lesson learned: The Aidens are tough and gifted, yes, but challenging in many respects.

Aiden is probably going to be a scientist.

UNDERESTIMATE

Alli was another of those who was just waiting to blossom. Alli had the ability to do well academically and speaking. She just needed encouragement. Alli blossomed on one of the best Quick Recall teams I ever coached. She also bloomed in front of the school one day, giving a speech. It was one of those defining moments.

Lesson learned: Be on the lookout for those children who are just waiting to blossom.

I hope Alli becomes a teacher. Something special about her could work miracles.

WHY?

Adyla was a beautiful child of a dear friend of mine. She made me think actress, because she had that natural charm. She could laugh with the best of them. She also was an excellent athlete. A play came to town and tryouts were held. I convinced her to try out. Well, a lot of the other kids had experience. She had no prior experience, and was not chosen. She was brokenhearted. Naturally, I felt heartbroken because I had encouraged her to take the chance. The next day, I knew I had to talk to her. She came to the hallway with tears in her eyes, asking me why I put her up to trying out for the play. I answered, "Had you rather me not push you to try new things?" Needless to say I felt pretty bad.

Lesson learned: Be careful. All children are different. Be sure of their talents. Your hunches, events, and experiences shape each one differently.

I have a feeling she will be a coach.

WOW

Graham was probably one of the most gifted students I have had in class, academics-wise. Graham had no trouble in any subject area, and I mean *any* area. He was just plain old smart. He was one of the best players at Quick Recall, and he excelled at academic tests. Being so gifted is great, but also tough because no one wants to be around someone who is that good. The kids were a little tough on Graham, which goes with the territory. Everyone in the district knew Graham.

Lesson learned: Being so gifted is great, yet it can be hard on a student. I know Graham is making the big bucks, wherever he is now.

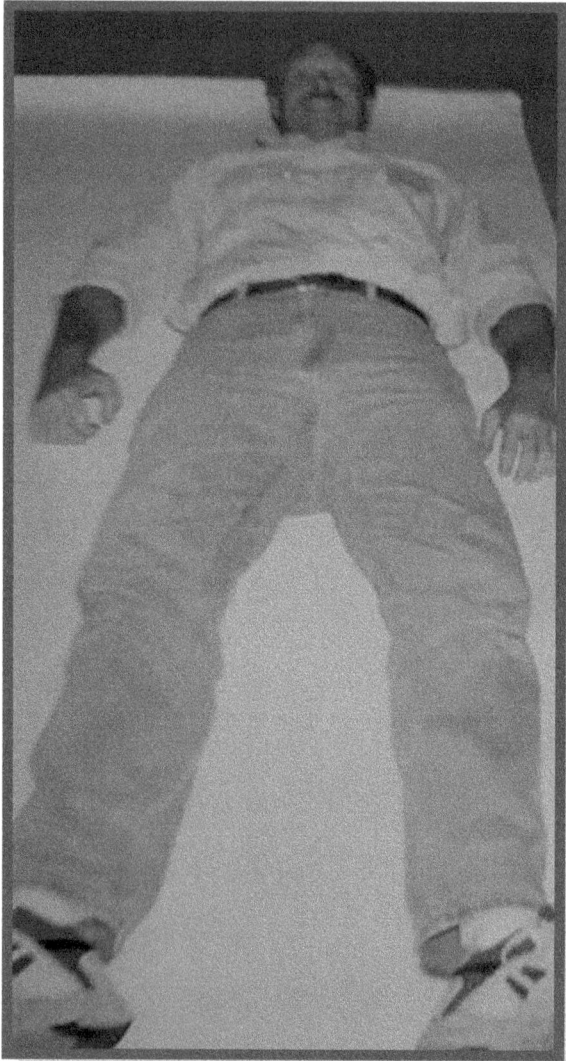

YOU NEVER KNOW

Kyle was one of those kids you note because he had reddish hair and freckles. Kyle was the type of student who really just mainstreamed. No trouble, no standing out, just blending into the mix real well. I suppose Kyle liked my style of teaching. However, you just never know what will happen in life. I was in the theater in Hopkinsville one day and Kyle came up to me. He had become a PE teacher. I taught alongside Kyle in my later years, and he referred to me as his mentor. Of course everyone had a good laugh at that.

Lesson learned: You never know what kids get from you or where they will end up.

Today Kyle is a PE teacher and a dang good one at that, willing to dress as a woman, sleep on a roof, sumo wrestle, and do the extras as a teacher.

I am proud to be called his mentor.

YOUR OWN

Katie is the third of three children, and unfortunately the first two were both good at everything. Top athletics and academics, and also Student Council presidents. A lot of hard acts to follow. Katie totally surprised her own dad in a book competition. She designed a musical tin can story box. I had never seen anything like it. Katie had the talent; She just decided when she would use it. In fact, Katie graduated from college having hardly cracked a book, just listening in class.

Lesson learned: Beneath your very own eyes is a child that will amaze you if they want to.

Katie tried the business world, but she filed her papers to become a guidance counselor.

YOU THINK SO

I will never forget taking Lib to my school. It was one of those schools loaded with talent. I remember her saying, "I'll never be like those kids." Boy, was she right, but not in the way she thought. She carved a road that included four Prom Queen appointments, sports, GSP, and getting chosen as Miss Wildcat. Yet for all of Lib's accomplishments, she is so special and kind to others, especially her sister. I always left Lib notes about how proud I was of her.

Lesson learned: If children underestimate their potential, they have no idea what can unfold.

My wish for Lib, the life of a lifetime.

James Redd is a retired elementary and gifted/talented teacher where he taught in many school districts in Western Kentucky. He guided himself in being unconventional and prided himself to find unique and creative ways to teach his students based on caring and mutual respect.

He coached Odyssey of the Mind, Academic, and Stock Market Teams where his students and teams received many state awards.

This book reflects what his kids taught him along the way as well as observing his peers and the teaching profession in general. The book is based upon his love for the art of teaching, beyond any profession.

www.ingramcontent.com/pod-product-compliance
Lightning Source LLC
Chambersburg PA
CBHW052119030426
42335CB00025B/3058